UNDERSTANDING

THE

STEPS TO

LEADERSHIP

Part. 1

RE-DISCOVERING THE FORCE BEHIND LEADING AND THE ATTITUDE THAT INFLUENCES HUMAN ACTIONS

EPHRAIM Igwe

TABLE OF CONTENT

- Becoming effective leader.

- How to listen to your inner voice

- How to think like professional leaders

- Becoming a leader

- Discovering the you in you

- How to master and manifest your potential

- Price of true Leadership

- How to gain access to kingdom wealth

Discovering the leader within you.

And many more.

DEDICATION

Just as it takes more than a village to raise a child, so it takes the collaboration of many individuals to achieve greater success. This book is the number one product of a corporate effort. I give you all the credit for guiding me to bring this to the world. I hope that this book will help you fund the missing link in leadership and that you will live to express it in your lifetime.

This book is dedicated to my beloved mother, Evangelist Igwe P. The General overseas of New Resurrection Christ Assembly Int.

You are the backbone of this great achievement, thank you for trusting me. You played a vital motherly role.

To all of my students all over the world, who have read many of my books on leadership and are eager for more

To you all who want to excel in leadership and business development. To all of my university friends and colleagues who supported me in a variety of ways when i was putting this project together. I hope that you will find in this book the true intent of God for your life

INTRODUCTION

Whether you are the CEO of a large corporation, a teacher, a home-maker, an artist, a construction worker, the owner of a small business, a government worker, a farmer, a doctor, a student or any other vocation or position in life: The self—discovery of the inherent leadership reality and an understanding of who you are and what you are meant to be are the key to successful living.

All my life I have seek to understand what the missing link in leadership is and why many never become it. But I understood that the secret is not about power, or our level of education but just as the life hidden inside a seed is brought forth when the seed is placed in the right soil or environment. So the true spirit of leadership is made alive when purpose is rightly discovered and cultivated.

This book is the answer whom you have sought for years. Let's consider the fascinating story of a Shepherd somewhere in Africa. As he demonstrated the missing link in our leadership development.

There was once a shepherd. Who has many sheep that he could let them out to find pasture on a daily basis. One day he brought his sheep out to pasture as usual, and while they were grazing, he suddenly heard a strange sound from the grass.

And due to his curiosity he wanted to know what it might be, but it turned out to be a young lion, clearly separated from his family. His first thought was of the danger he would face if he stayed close to the young lion and his parents return.

He quickly left the area and watched from a distance to see if the mother lion would return. But she couldn't. until the sun began to set, and there was still no way to protect the young lion. He then decided to take him home and care for him.

He hand-fed the young lion for about six months with milk and kept him He was safe and secure under the protective house he built for his sheep.

As the young lion progresses from a newborn stage to a certain degree, he decides to take him out with the other sheep daily to feed from the bushes around the village.

The Lion has become a sheep by societal norms and tradition.

He has slightly slipped away from his real innate position and become like one of them. That even at a grown-up stage, the lion still think like a sheep.

Then, four years later. He evolved into an adolescent lion, but he acted, sounded, responded, and behaved like his sheep association, and his sheep club, recognized him as one of their member, and they never knew what he was and what he was capable of. Because of how he has given up on his ideals and accepted the sheep's normal life.

Now, the shepherd sat on a rock in four years during the winter months of the year, taking refuge in the smoky shadow of a leafless tree. watching his flock as they waded into the calm, flowing water of a canal called the river of life for water. Suddenly, just across the river, a huge beast emerged from the thick jungle bush that the lion had never seen before.

THE HUGE BEAST ACROSE THE RIVER

The sheep panicked and leapt out of the water and ran toward the sheep house, as if under the influence of some survival instinct they could get refuge. So they run as fast as possible and never stopped but nodded their heads as they were all running with the young lion to huddled in the pen's fence.

The situation was so terrifying to them, so that the young lion run ahead of many sheep for fear, even though he is becoming mature but he was also huddled with them, stricken with great fear. As the beast made that great rumbling sound that seemed to shake the entire forest, the flock scrambled for shelter.

The shepherd lifted up his head and saw what he had in his blood-drenched mouth, the lifeless body of a lamb from the flock, as he lifted his head above the tall grass. The man recognized that danger had returned to his side of the forest.

After one week of being untouched, the young lion went down to the river to drink as usual, and then, as the flock grazed. He immediately bent over the pool, panicked and ran wildly toward the sheep-house for safety.

The sheep did not run and wondered why he had done so, while the lion wondered why the sheep had not run since seeing the beast again. After a while, the young lion returned slowly to the flock and then to the pool to drink again. He saw the beast once more and froze in agony. It was his own reflection in the water but he didn't know.

TRY THIS AND BECOME ONE OF US

While he tried to understand what he was seeing, suddenly, the beast appeared out of the jungle again. The flock dashed with breakneck speed toward the sheep-house, but before the young lion could move, the beast stepped in the water toward him and made that deafening sound that filled the forest.

For a moment, the young lion felt that his life has gone. He realized that he saw not just one beast, but about three right there in the water of life, one before him and two in his back.

His head was filled with confusion because of the angry beast that was coming, just about ten feet from him. At this point, he didn't know what to do. He now decided to stand still as the beast began to growl at him, face—to—face with a frightening voice in a way that seemed to say to him, "try this and be transformed like us".

TRY THIS AND BE TRANSFORMED LIKE US. But the more the beast growled at him the more frightening he became and the more frightening he became the more he became aware of himself, his—true nature, his—strength, and his ability as well as his true mind.

Now, he decided in that fear to make an exact sound whether he would appease them by so doing. But his own gaping jaws were a sound of the sheep. Then the beast started responding louder, as if to say, "yees, yes do it, I say do it again, continue, you are almost there" This continued till about five to six times finally, he burst into his true self and started making the same sound!

THE LION HAS BEGINNING TO EXPERIENCE CHANGE BY CHANGING HIS ASSOCIATION

At this point, he started developing a deep feeling of intensity that he had never felt before. He automatically started experiencing a total transformation, starting from his spirit-mind-to his body.

TRANSFORMATION FROM THE MIND

As he was still standing right there in the river of transfiguration, the three beasts started growling at each other. Then the Shepherd saw what he had never seen from birth and would never live to forget for life. As those beast filled the forest with their sound from about a mile away, the big beast stopped, turned his back on the little lion, and started moving towards the thick forest.

After two to three feet he paused and looked right where the young lion was standing one more time, and started growling, as if to say, "I hope you are coming with me?" the young lion knew what the signal meant and he started realizing that a day to decide his destiny now.

This came as a special invitation for the body of a lion to possess the spirit of a lion in the juggle.

The day to choose his destiny is here, whether to continue the fake life with the sheep or become the self that he had discovered. Now, many thoughts started coming to his mind.

TRUE LEADERSHIP IS BORN WHEN YOU DISCOVER A VISION THAT TRIGGERED YOU TO DECIDE YOUR DESTINY

As he noticed that, for him to embark on this journey, he would have to give up the safety that his master guaranteed him earlier. His daily bread, (The monthly salaries), the simple, predictable and fearful lifestyle of the sheep and enter the frightening, unpredictable jungle.

Indeed it was a day to make a choice, to pull off the false Image of another lifestyle and embrace the true image of his value and significance.

The most interesting part of this experience was that it served as an invitation for the body of the young lion to possess the spirit of a lion in the juggle. An invitation to a lion-in-sheep mentality to become the king of the jungle.

Then the young lion lifted up his head looking back and forth at the thick forest and the sheep farm and back to the big beast. After a few times, the big beast started growling and moving towards the thick forest again and the young lion completely turned his back on the sheep farm and the sheep whom he had lived with for years, and he followed the beast into the forest to become the king that the creator created him to be from the beginning

A day to decide your destiny

CHAPTER ONE

STEP AWAY FROM YOUR OLD IMAGE AND EMBRACE YOUR TRUE-SELF

Our future is a product of our mind.

What you believe about yourself, and alter in your thought create your destiny because they manifest in your attitude. Just as the leader within the young lion completely come alive when he turned his back on the sheep farm and the sheep whom he had lived with for years and crossed the river with the beast into the forest. Leaving behind his past life as a lion in sheep mentality and embarking on the life he was born to lead. So you must decide for yourself today. This book is a special invitation for you to step over your old image and embrace your true self.

You are the lion in the river, whom this book came to challenge to step across the river of fear and enter into the forest of effective leadership which the creator expected you to manifest.

to become the king that the creator created him to be from the beginning.

A call to decide your destiny!

Just as the young lion decided to growl back to the big beast that developed him to his true nature. So you will release the inherent leadership strength when you realize your true potential.

Just as the young lion lifted his head looking back and forth at the thick forest and the sheep farm and back to the big beast. And then decided to take that step so you need to decide to step forward. Knowing that he has a future to decide today.

You have a future to decide today!

As he looked back to the sheep farm where his old friends were and then looked towards the thick forest the position of his power, where the big lion was heading and decided to take that step, so you have to evaluate your past unprogressive—life and step across the river to your true potential.

Decide to step towards the thick forest like the young lion, who defies the fear of losing his assured safe, secure and civilized environment and to embark on the journey of entering the unpredictable and dangerous life of the jungle, you have to completely conclude losing your simple life if you are going to dive into a deeper realm of extraordinary leadership

You will release the hidden leader within you by responding to the great leader of all time Jesus Christ. Just as the young lion became dangerous by responded to the growl of the big beast and became transformed, into his real—self.

Immediately the young lion started growling back to the big beast, he started experiencing all over his body, something he never felt before. That is how you are going to feel when you evaluate and conclude from your heart that you are done with average life And then step forward into the extraordinary forest.

This is a critical process that is involved in capturing and manifesting your true—self. And this is the reason why it is so difficult for many individuals to embark on this transformation and transition, to cross the river of fear to their true selves. In fact, without this metamorphosis, no amount of leadership seminar, training, and education can get one transformed from normal to abnormal, from ordinary to extraordinary and from follower to the leading class

CHAPTER TWO

THE WAY FORWARD

Just as the young lion evaluated the gain he would get in the future over his past and decided to take a step toward the thick forest. So Peter, Andrew, James and the rest of the twelve, evaluated the gain they would get following Jesus rather than the old fishing company.

Think about the Ancient story of the children of Israel. Who by the reason of the land that Moses the man of God told them. Left their homes.

Moses demonstrated this in his writings. How he received a distinct assignment from God. He first, narrated the story of his encounter with God in the wilderness, wherein God revealed to him that his birth was intended to fulfil the task of guiding the people of Israel, who were slaves in Egypt, to the promised land.

This creates a strong confidence within him and the feeling of purpose drives him to become passionate about paying the ultimate price for this rescue quest. And by this strength of this vision he gave his fellow Israelites hope that they would be free to reach the promised land with him.

He went on to share this vision with his brother Aaron, who accompanied him to the children of Israel. Telling them that their freedom is possible, and giving them the hope of " A land flowing with honey"

Vision motivates leadership.

Vision is so powerful that people lose their comfort zone chasing what they

believe to be true.

Vision is the key to success

Vision is the best way to lead.

Vision is the best way to get to the top

Vision gives you an address to the journey of life!

It was by the strength of this vision of Moses that genuine conviction became inspired within them that they left their houses, businesses, jobs and schools in other to follow Moses to the land that he told them about.

These also happened in the life of Jesus the Christ. He inspired and motivated his followers to the point they left all, for the sake of following Jesus to the kingdom of God which he promised to everyone who believed in his name.

Moses had such a strong sense of purpose that it took—root and motivated others to start thinking that they, too, could achieve freedom. They were moved by Moses's enthusiasm to fearlessly depart Egypt and follow him into the desert, where there was no sign of civilization no money, no food, or clean water instead of returning to their familiar and agonizing life as prisoners and labourers in Egypt.

The place that Moses, the man of God, had told them about was worth risking everything for. Keep this in mind

CHAPTER THREE

HOW TO STEP INTO YOUR TRUE NATURE

Converted attitude is the root of genuine transformation from the mind!

Until complete change happened in the mind the lion was still thinking, acting, responding and living in fear like the sheep that he has become by association. Instead of revealing the king of the jungle.

"You are the light of the world, and a city that is set on a hill that cannot be hidden" the Bible says.

You are a leader.

You release the hidden leader within you by responding to the great leader of all time Jesus Christ.

Just as the young lion became dangerous by responded back to the growl of the big beast and became transformed, into his real—self.

The hug beast across the river is Jesus and he is standing right behind the door of your heart, knocking if by chance you would open to him, that he may lead you to the thick forest of glorious fulfillment.

His leadership and inspirational statement serve as a special invitation to humanity, and to everyone who desires the position of leadership.

This is the fundamental key to everyone who wants to go into leadership. As the big lion stood growling at the young lion, so Jesus sat with the twelve that he had chosen to train as leaders. The growling is like saying, " look, heah, I'm here to introduce you to yourself" .

This is how Jesus introduced the twelve to themselves and sent them, to heal deliver and perform miracles.

IF YOU ARE NOT TRAINED YOU WILL NEVER LEAD

Imagine a fisherman healing a leper and commanding miracles for, the first time in the history of man. The transformation has taken place, starting from the mind, spirit and then the body. When Jesus walked on the water, he said, "You can do this too" "Come" the biblical account that a mortal man walks on the water. He heals the sick and says,

"Greater than this are possible to you because I'm going to the father" What manner of man is this? Who has a solution to every problem?

Apostle Paul was blessing the communion in Corinthian Eleven. Here he said, " For I have received of the Lord that which also I delivered unto you, That the Lord Jesus the same night in which he was betrayed took bread:1 Corinthians 11:23

In other words, i learn all I'm teaching you from my master. It is never my doctrine but the master.

Jesus is that big lion growling at you, face to face. Saying, "Come on, step forward. You can do this" Come unto me, all ye that labour and are heavy laden, and I will give you rest." Matthew 11:28

You are a young lion, have not also read that God is the lion of the tribe of Judi-a.

Jesus is the one saying "Follow me", and I will make you Fisher of men". So, therefore,

1. it is time to evaluate the cost and gain. To step toward with him or to remain in our current life.

2. It is time to refuse to die in your current position but make a difference.

3. It is time to choose where you will spend your future.

4. It is time you make decisions for your future.

5. It is time to step forward to what you believe.

6. It is time to emerge from the dark forest of life.

7. It is time to choose where you will spend your eternity.

8.. You can do better.

Develop a professional leadership mindset

Those who join the military are first sent to boot camp, where they are trained and mentored to think like professional military men.

Though they were formally civilians thinking like civilians, they were oriented to think professionally like soldiers at the time. First and foremost, they are separated from their families, friends, and the rest of society to concentrate on new assignments.

Think about David who delivered the children of Israel from the hands of the Philippines giant. You can never manifest true leadership except you withdraw yourself from the crowd.

As a young shepherd boy, David was isolated from families and friends for many years in the forest, but he never saw it as suffering; rather, the experience he gained in the forest while fighting with Lions and wolves gave him the courage to believe and step forward for the deliverance of his people Israel.

Without a doubt, he was the only one who truly believed that the Israelites could defeat their enemies, including the great Philistine warrior.

Goliath of Gat, whose coat of mail alone weighed two hundred pounds.

His passion for his purpose after his anointing, even at such a young age, inspired others who shared his vision. Before revealing his leadership abilities, he inquired! "What shall be done to the man who killeth this Philistine and removes the reproach from Israel?"

Who is this uncircumcised Philistine to defy the armies of the living God?" Samuel 17:26. We long for leaders who think professionally like David rather than the most powerful leader with a slave mentality

CHAPTER FOUR

THE MINDSET THAT MAKES A LEADER

Converted attitude is rooted in genuine transformation.

An invitation for the body to enter into his spiritual position of power.

Just Immediately the young lion started growling back to the big beast, he started experiencing all over his body, something he never felt before. That is how you are going to feel when you evaluate and conclude from your heart that you are done with your average life. Then you will step into the extraordinary. You can build your own company instead of complaining about who pays you or doesn't pay.

This message is a special invitation for you and me to tap into our true nature. Leaders are typically ordinary people who have been thrust into extraordinary situations. Some men tried to review, and use their gift to promote humanity; and by doing so, they created a character within themselves that inspires confidence and trust in those who believe.

Who is a leader?

You are the only one that can change your current condition and this must begin from your mind.

In essence, no amount of training, education, and qualifications can make an effective leader. Until true transformation took place in the realm of the mind. They can never be a true transition. So, this is an invitation, for an ordinary to emerge extraordinary.

It is a call for a follower to experience his true nature. This came as an opportunity for you to decide your Destiny. Note that he never forced him to make a choice, he only created suspense in his mind and left him to decide. Whether to take the step with him or remain in his lost condition.

Many people are lost while living

The big beast only came to introduce the young lion to himself. And then left him to decide. You can imagine the big beast growling face to face with the young lion who was filled with great fear.

This is like the rich telling the poor "Step up with me. You too can achieve all this". Don't look down on yourself. You are a lion.

CHAPTER FIVE

SPECIAL INVITATION TO THE POSITION OF INFLUENCE

Leadership is influence: Genuine leadership is a product of influence! genuine influence is the key to effective leadership. This started from inspiration, you can imagine how the big beast inspired the young lion to step into his true self.

The most significant lesson in this fascinating story is that, in the same way the Big Beast influenced the young lion he decided after a while to follow him to the thicker part of the forest, so Jesus influenced his followers to follow him regardless of the pain it might cost them.

With a promise to lead them to the place of rest, he promised everyone who believed in his name.

Genuine influence is not a result of memorizing formulas, learning skills or imitating methods it is an attitude that

grew from the heart. This comes as you start discovering who you are and what you are capable of doing.

At some point mother bird will nudge her baby birds out of the nest, as if to say "You need to do what you were born to do" and they will either start flying or risk falling out of the nest.

Is like a father advising his son, saying,

" you need to start up something for yourself because you can't be a child forever" The same is true for you in the sense that you truly want to overcome incredible odds.

And step into the forest of your power, where you will be given a rightto reign as King instead of a follower. In essence, you are a King but you must become.

1. Every King used to be a follower.

2. Every King brings into the world his gift.

3. Every King has a place of power.

4. Every King has a domain of authority.

Every King needs a domain. The reason why many people have been finding it difficult to birth their dreams is because they are in the wrong domain. This is why the most critical war among men is the war of freedom. Because they need a place of their power. This is like having the most expensive car in the world without a good road.

The principle of effective leadership is

1. Vision. You are not a leader until you discover a vision for your life.

2. Purpose. You are not a leader until you master

CHAPTER SIX

MAN's GREATEST IGNORANT

I have learned that man's greatest ignorance is himself. And if you don't know your self you will never understand your purpose! This is why the scripture says, love your neighbour as you love yourself. Jesus said this because we all have gone astray and looking at his kind of leadership, Jesus manifested true love. He went to the cross because of the love he has for humanity and makes us understand that a genuine effective leader can not be born without true love.

Though people have abused the system that is why our social media platforms and daily news no longer spend a day without displaying a critical dilemma. We hear of financial fraud when national presidents and members of their cabinet are being prosecuted by their governments.

Priests who abuse their power to exploit the people they were sworn to serve a common sight. What about the business executives that are succumbing to corruption by the dozen? What then can the youths who are motivated to take the candle and step forward do?

MAN'S GREATEST IGNORANT IS HIMSELF.

A careful study of the story that opened this discussion will understand how the young Lion who lost connection with his parents and was forced by circumstances to live and associate with sheep for survival, ended up growing up with the sheep mentality.

He thought he was a sheep and was in that condition for years till he came to a point of decision where he either had to become his true self or forever in an organization that was not designed for him. Many people are currently in this situation, they are in a relationship, marriage, job and office that was not designed for them.

The young Lion was comfortable with the situation till the day of the decision, he looked back to the sheep's house his previous life where his security, daily bread and monthly salary were guaranteed him. And towards the forest where he was going to lose it all in other to develop into his true nature. Then, he decided "I'm going to embark on this journey no matter what it may cost me".

He followed the Great Beast into the thickest part of the forest and was restored to himself, his destiny and his place of power. This exact challenge is inputted by Jesus Christ for Humanity—restoration to their place of Dominion.

"And he said to them all If any man will come after me, let him deny himself, and take up his cross daily, and follow me.

For whosoever will save his life shall lose it: but whosoever will lose his life for my sake, the same shall save it.

For what is a man advantaged, if he gains the whole world, and loses himself, or is cast away?"
Luke 9:23-25

The death of Jesus on the cross declared to us that despite humanity's declaring independence from our source and sustainer which leads many to manifest tragic and evil rebellious results, God hasn't changed his mind on who he made us to be from creation and the purpose for our design. He passionately through Jesus committed to our being reconnected to him. Because of three powerful reasons.

1. His purpose is always permanent; whatever he set out to do, he must surely do it.

2. We were designed in his image and likeness and he doesn't want his image to be destroyed or disgraced in the world.

3. His love for us is eternal!

Reconnection

The fall of man started with a disobedient to the word of God. Words are very powerful and the reason behind the loss of the young Lion was a result of being disconnected from the word of his parents. So when man disobeyed the word of God he was disconnected from the Spirit of God, who would enable them to towards their destiny. And because of the disconnection, they had no other place to get their thoughts from, and since they were left with no choice, they got them from their environment. This is what man has been living on for over a thousand years. His thoughts, the deceitfulness of his adversary.

RESTORATION THROUGH THE WORLD

The scripture says, " He sends forth his word and heals them "

Just as the big Lion growls face to face with the young Lion the creator is growling to humanity calling for a reconnection.

The only thing some people are sure of is death.

Death is the only thing an average person can be certain of, a loss of one's sense of meaning in life. Many people have developed self-hatred, deception, self-denying the truth about oneself, lying to oneself, fear of failure, fear of failure, fear of the unknown, and a general fear of others around them as a result of ignorance, ignorance of personal identity, ignorance of personal responsibility, ignorance of personal purpose, and ignorance of purpose. we were not created to be different from the rest of the world.

What does it mean to be successful

The fact that you still boast about your car and your little accomplishments signifies that you are still lost.

Just like the young lion who lost his identity and his sense of value and normalized life in a strange average kingdom, pretending to be something when he was nothing, pretending to be something. He was reintroduced to himself by a special invitation from his true kingdom, which led to his freedom. Many people are like this lion. Even when we are cured, we will often try to argue about or even the normal life that we have accepted to be normal to us. (Do you know that i am the owner of an oil company?) Then we begin to count our little accomplishments, what does it mean to be successful in life?

CHAPTER SEVEN

THE PART OF LEADERSHIP

Iron sharpeneth iron; so a man sharpeneth the countenance of his friend. Proverbs 27:17

just as the young Lion saw the older Lion and recognized his true self and decided to reconnect back to his true nature, but the process of his growth was still ahead of him. He recognized his identity, but he had to understand what that identity meant for him. Only by following the big beast to the right environment for him. That is the only way he can take his place and position as a king. The same is true for us all, if we must make it to the position of our destiny, and leadership as well as life. We must come to the point where we will accept and recognize with anticipation and passion to step forward with kings class.

BEING AWARE OF OUR LEADERSHIP IS AWARENESS WE NEED THE MENTALITY OF A LEADER.

Having the information of our leadership is just awareness we need the mentality too otherwise, we will return to our previous condition. There should be a complete transformation from our minds. Our minds matter because they control how we manage every matter. You can imagine how the young Lion responded the first time the big Lion growled at him, expecting him to growl back as a Lion but his sound was like a sheep.

Lion Responding Like A Sheep

Lion growling like a sheep. He has normalized the situation and would have remained there till death. But as the big Lion began to growl heavier, he suddenly developed into his true nature and true identity as well as his true sense. That compelled him to agree with the big Lion that could lead him to his place of destiny and fulfilment.

Something happened to his mind, that led his body to the environment that was designed for him. Something happened to his mind that led him to cross over to the other side of the forest. He had an encounter that produced strong conviction otherwise he could have returned to the sheep environment.

THERESE A DEEPER RELATIONSHIP BETWEEN LEADERSHIP ABILITY AND LEADERSHIP MENTALITY

This is a great challenge to everyone interested in the position of leadership.

No wonder Apostle Paul said, "Be renewed in the spirit of your mind" Note that Paul was talking to people who have received the word of God and have accepted to follow Jesus. Paul was indicating that they had not fully changed in the way they needed to do.

That we are a Leader of many organizations doesn' t mean we are thinking like professional leaders, and if you don' t develop thinking like professional leaders you will never remain in a position of power.

Those who develop a professional leadership mindset are leaders for life

CHAPTER EIGHT

LEADERSHIP IS SELF DISCOVERY

Two things happen when you want to exercise leadership, (1) you must realize that you are inherently a Leader.

(2) you must develop a certain kind of thinking, and leadership mentality.

who you are and who you think you are is the prerequisite for leadership. Leadership is about discovering your identity as one born a leader and then understanding the way effective leaders think so that you can live to the fullest as a leader. You need to first establish your leadership mindset, otherwise it will be difficult for you to remain a Leader all your life.

Effective leaders are concerned with who you are rather than what you do. This is the reason why leadership actions flow naturally from their inherent ability.

Therefore, to exercise leadership you must believe that you are created to lead.

To pursue purpose, you must think like a leader. You must have the leader's thoughts, to have the thoughts of leadership you must have an encounter with your inherent nature, true self.

Just as the young Lion saw the big beast and recognised himself and was left with no option but to follow that self that he had encountered!

Just as a newborn baby can not give himself a name except the parent.

Just as a product cannot give itself a name no understand its purpose except with its relationship with the maker so you must be restored and reconciled to God in other to understand your true purpose and true ability.

CHAPTER NINE

THE MISSING INGREDIENTS IN LEADERSHIP

As we read earlier in the story that triggered us to engulf into the study of the mystery behind the missing ingredient in leadership development.

The young Lion who was completely separated from his parents and was forced by circumstances to live in a strange kingdom that was designed for a sheep. A Government's that was designed for sheep and his prime ministers, regulated by sheep mentality.

THE LION HAS BECOME A SHEEP BY ASSOCIATION

He gradually lost the sense of his purpose, sense of his—value and sense of meaning in his life and was left with no choice but to accept the negative and fake life that the situation imposed on him. But a day came when he encountered himself and was challenged to re-discover and manifest his true self.

He experienced what he had never seen or felt in his body and this became his motivation that he made up his mind to follow the big beast to the thickest forest.

GODS ULTIMATE PURPOSE FOR MAN

This fascinating story is a deep mystery of the loss of man in the world and the idea of God's ultimate restoration for the disconnected body of a man to re-discover the true spirit of leadership called the Holy Spirit.

The Holy Spirit is the missing ingredient in leadership and must be re-discovered in other to manifest our true nature.

The Holy Spirit is a Leader according to Paul in his letter to the church in Galatians 5:26 But if ye be led of the Spirit, ye are not under the law.

Now the works of the flesh are manifest, which are these; Adultery, fornication, uncleanness, lasciviousness,

Idolatry, witchcraft, hatred, variance, emulations, wrath, strife, seditions, heresies,

Envyings, murders, drunkenness, revellings, and such like: of the which I tell you before, as I have also told you in time past, that they which do such things shall not inherit the kingdom of God.

But the fruit of the Spirit is love, joy, peace, longsuffering, gentleness, goodness, faith,

Meekness, temperance: against such there is no law. And they that are Christ's have crucified the flesh with the affections and lusts. Let us not be desirous of vain glory, provoking one another, envying one another.

What is ingredient

Ingredients refer to the qualities a Leader must cultivate for his effectiveness. These include.

Purpose

Vision

Passion

Love

Integrity

Truthfulness

Faithfulness

Fearlessness

Discipline

Self-control

Self-discovery

Humility

the Spirit of teamwork.

Attitude

Selflessness

Character!

Title, position, power, fame, wealth, family name and influence cannot make you a true leader. This is reason why, if you hire a person for your company for instance; you will give him all the titles, a staff and every other things. But he will be limited in taking initiative. In fact he can't try to solve any problems by himself or seek a better ways of performing tasks. He just does exactly as he's told and doesn't destroy old policy or methods. That's not leadership in as much as the management is pushing the boundaries.

Leadership has become a name and a role people play rather than a life they lead. This is because we sit in the position of leadership but our attitude is still displaying sheep character. These for me, is so because, we are lion but were mentored by sheep. That is why we always go back to our normal life.

The lion attitude.

The lion attitude is what distinguish a leader from followers. We must therefore capture and cultivate the spirit of our true attitude. Imagine a lion who eat sheep for his daily meal was converted to agree to live together with sheep because he has been trained to abandon his real attitude and has been cultured with sheep attitude. The lion was so lost that even the day he meet his true image he conclude that his life has come to an end.

The only thing ignorant people are sure of is death. They live unreasonable life and still pray to continue living.

WHAT IS ATTITUDE

Our attitude is a product of a behaviour and character that we accept to be true to us. These stems from a perception of whom we are. It is a learned behavior, which control the way we see ourselves and the world.

TRUE LEADERS DOESN'T LIVE IN EXCUSES

The Lion who lost his original attitude was numbered as one of the sheep by association. This system is applied to you and I when we lost our original attitude we became like one of the slaves.

The problem is that the young Lion has never admitted that he needs help, just like you and I. We always have a way of giving excuses rather than performance.

CHAPTER TEN

WHAT MAKES A LEADER

The question is when did this one become a leader? Some people think leadership is by titles, educational qualifications, position of power, financial level or skill. But none of all these things is the prerequisite for leadership.

Leadership is not by size but attitude

It doesn't matter how many certificates you have or did not have the truth is that inside you is a hidden Leader; but you must become a leader.

Can you still realize how powerful the Lion is. But he was brainwashed to accept that he was a sheep and the sheep who were supposed to be afraid of him, became his masters, the Lion has become a subject to his circumstances. The same to all human. We are all victims of unfulfilled passion for greatness, we want to become better but we don't have the passion to step forward. We want to change our current job by creating our own business but we are afraid of failing.

Leadership begins with a self discovery

I have seen undergraduate who employed more than 50 graduate. I have also seen a lame who can not walk but has a company employing people. This is to make you understand that leadership is not ability nor about power but mentality.

You must therefore train yourself to thinking like professional leaders if you must remain a leader. Leaders think different because of what they discovered about whom they were.

Nelson Mandela

Mandela's life purpose was to end segregation or discrimination based on race in south africa, as well as the promotion of racial equality. He wished for a democratic society open to all people, both black and white. His drive for his purpose compelled him to step forward and fight as a way to achieve his goal. For this, he was sentenced to life in prison, but he reaffirmed his country's vision during his sentencing hearing.

"I have fought against white domination, and i have fought against black domination, according to him. I have adored the idea of a democratic and free society in which all people live in harmony and with equal opportunities. I want to live for and achieve it, but it will be difficult if necessary. I am able to die if i have an idea". The same is true with you if you must become effective leader. You must deny your self and take up the cross of serving your gift to humanity at all cost.

David

David is one of the most fascinating and influential figures in the bible and the world. He concentrated on serving his god, restoring his nation's glory, and defending his people politically and militarily. As a young shepherd boy, he was so passionate about his purpose. And daily striving toward it right after his anointing. He was the only one who believed that the israelites could defeat their adversary. Goliath.

David became a military hero and was a favorite in the courts of king soul, whose son jonathan became his mentor. Yet. certainly. David succes' time on the battlefield set up a long and arduous decade of conflict and exile for him. Saul and his loyal followers were frantically running for their lives as he attempted to kill him in jealousy. Saul and his son jonathan were killed in a battle against the philistines, and david took over as king, but only under david's rule. Israel's destiny was decided when it became one of the world's most respected, feared, and powerful nations. David story is a great motivation to all of us. A Shepherd boy coming to take over the highest national president office all because of self discovery.

You are a leader. You are a chief controller design not to dominate others but serve them with you gift.

•All the things you see happening all around the world is motivated by people like you who discovered whom they are and choose to serve them to the world.

•You don't supposed to leave the world the same way you meet it.

•A you can become is already in you, but you can discover them when you discover the word of God concerning you.

• Finally, my brethren, we discover our fullest ability, capacity, Power, value, honor, and place of Dominion by discovering Jesus and the kingdom of our God.

CHAPTER ELEVEN

A SENSE OF PURPOSE

Leadership effectiveness is largely dependent on having a clear sense of purpose, which gives one's life's work and gives others around them a

unique sense of meaning to their own life.

Without a well-defined goal, effective leadership management cannot be born, developed, or implied anywhere in the world. For this reason, every one of the ancient leaders is well-known for their actions, which turn into

their passions.

The word "purpose" here, refers to learning the motivation behind something and is correctly defined as the main goal or intent behind something's creation.

Effective leadership is born out of a purpose, which instils in its followers a strong sense of dedication and passion to achieve their goals at any cost. In other words, having a purpose gives one a goal-oriented mindset, driving

by a vision of a future that is better than the present.

We naturally want to go after something, or become better than we are. That is why many keep changing jobs. And demanding for a better kind of jobs. Some have also changed many relationship to another seeking a better kind of it, because when you don't know the purpose for even what you have received already, abuse is inevitable. That's true. When you don't know what something is for, there is no doubt, you must disvalue therefore the amount of value you place on something depends on your knowledge of it. And so people has loose their marriages, jobs, positions and offices

because of insufficient knowledge of what they have.

PURPOSE PRODUCE STRONG PASSION AND COURAGE

Let talk a little bit about biblical Queen Esther.

After accepting her role as a leader, Queen Esther developed a passion for it and was prepared to put her own life in danger to see it through. "If I perish, I perish," she declared. The king agreed to the plan to protect and free the Jews because of her strong courage. They were therefore motivated by her bravery to put their trust in her as a leader to protect

them from their enemies and stand up for them before the king.

She strategically influenced others because she had such a clear sense of

her purpose and leadership destiny.

That caused her to develop a passion for it that she was prepared to die for. The king was affected and influenced by this passion and bravery in ineffective leadership, which ultimately saved the entire country of Israel. Esther is prepared to accept death as a possibility because she is so

concerned about her people's freedom.

CHAPTER TWELVE

EXTRAORDINARY LEADERSHIP

Leadership is often associated with individuals who possess exceptional qualities and skills. However, it is not always the case that leaders are born with these attributes. Sometimes, leadership emerges from the most unexpected sources, such as in the story of Colin, a young boy who defied the odds and became an extraordinary leader after reading one of my book. We are going to delve into his inspiring journey, and highlight the qualities and experiences that shaped him into the remarkable leader he is today which he explained to me in one of my dialogues with him.

From a young age, Colin displayed a natural curiosity and an insatiable hunger for knowledge. He was always asking questions, seeking to understand the world around him. His parents recognized this thirst for learning and encouraged him to explore various interests. This early exposure to diverse experiences ignited a spark within Colin, laying the

groundwork for his future leadership development.

Nurturing Empathy

Colin's empathetic nature was evident in his interactions with others. He possessed an innate ability to empathize with people's struggles and emotions, which allowed him to connect with individuals from all walks of life. Whether it was comforting a friend in distress or supporting a classmate facing difficulties, Colin's compassionate spirit became a defining

characteristic of his leadership style.

* The Power of Mentorship

As Colin grew older, he lay his hand in one of my book on leadership titled THE REAL YOU. According to him, that compelled him to recognize the importance of mentorship and the profound impact it could have on an individual's growth. He then sought out mentors who could guide him on his path to leadership, whether it was a teacher, a community leader, or even an older sibling. These mentors provided Colin with invaluable guidance, support, and wisdom, shaping his

understanding of leadership and inspiring him to become a mentor himself.

* Courage in the Face of Adversity

Leadership often requires the courage to confront challenges and push through adversity. Colin faced his fair share of obstacles, but he never shied away from them. Whether it was standing up against injustice, advocating for marginalized communities, or challenging the status quo, Colin's unwavering determination and fearlessness propelled him forward. His ability to confront adversity head-on and inspire others to do the same set

him apart as an extraordinary leader.

* Inspiring Change, One Step at a Time

Colin's leadership journey extended beyond personal growth; it was driven by a deep desire to make a positive impact on his community and the world. He recognized that even the smallest actions could lead to significant change. Whether it was organizing community clean-up drives, volunteering at local shelters, or spearheading awareness campaigns, Colin's commitment to serving others and effecting change was unwavering.

Leadership is not confined to age or experience; it can emerge from the most unexpected individuals. Colin's story exemplifies this notion, as he defied societal expectations and grew into an extraordinary leader. His insatiable curiosity, empathetic nature. In fact, this can be an answer to everyone who seeks how to lead his people, family, business and public

organization as well as the government.

CHAPTER THIRTEEN

SELF DENIAL.

The major conditions in the Leadership development process are a...

1. You must deny yourself and submit to the mentoring of a master

2. You must accept the office of a servanthood.

3. Accept to serve or use your gifts at every opportunity.

4. The nature of true Leadership is the cultivation of a hardworking attitude.

Apostle Paul in his second letter to Timothy made a very touching statement, saying

"There are not only gold and silver vessels in a great house, but also wood and

earthen vessels, some honorable and some dishonorable," he said in closing.

"If a man, therefore, purges himself of these, he shall be a vessel unto honor,

sanctified and meet for the masters use and prepared unto every good work."

This is a powerful statement since true passion is based on understanding the

importance and purpose of our calling.

This is why when you know why you are doing something you become passionate about achieving their objectives! Others are enthused and

motivated to pursue the same objective because of this passion.

People are then naturally inspired, and this has an impact on their attitudes.

behaviours, and overall way of thinking and living.

True leadership passion, then, originates from the process of discovering a

belief.

Effective leadership is expensive and strong because it requires a clear understanding of one's conviction that the world needs the gift that is

hidden or trapped inside each of us.

Effective leadership is an outward manifestation of the inner ideas.

By this I consider effective leaders as people who successfully share their inner passions and inspire others to feel the same way. This is accurate because great leaders captivate people with their passion rather than chasing or pleading for followers. How did you suppose they drew in other people if this weren't the case? They draw people to them and inspire them to act

because of their passion.

They are frequently common people who choose the role of a servant rather than accepting the office of a high chief. In other words, they dedicate themselves to serving their community well, for which they were rewarded and recognize as their leaders. David the little shepherd boy is a prime

example of this.

David was an ordinary man whose extraordinary circumstances revealed his latent leadership potentials. This gave rise to the person who served as Saul the King's inspiration as well. That he agreed to bestow his confidence on him

to save the children of Israel.

This is the reason why great historical leaders were viewed as "victims" of their circumstances. That is to say, the demands of life awakes the sleeping

giant within them eventhough they had no intention of being great or lead.

WE CAN TAP INTO THE DEEPEST REALM OF

LEADERSHIP WHEN

WE LEARN TO THINK LIKE PROFESSIONAL LEADERS.

Professional leadership is required in our public offices, businesses, communities, and government. However, it's getting harder to find a real

one.

Leadership is not a label but performance

Every Human is driven by the need to become great and to be in a position of authority where they can rule and control situations. But unfortunately, many

mistake leadership for the capacity to manipulate others' needs and emotions.

True leadership, on the other hand, is demonstrated by performance and

outcomes rather than the titles or labels.

Leadership is not a label but performance

Genuine leaders that it takes a privilege to lead others. Change in our society

will result from a thorough comprehension of this.

Why do we need leadership?

In diverse situations, we need leadership to navigate and resolve difficulties, crises, and poverty by guiding the people to meet their aspirations. In most

cases, someone takes the lead, and step the people forward.

Leadership is not an ability but a mentality.

Leadership is one of the fundamental components of human nature according to the order of creation, it is inherent in all people, but adopting the mindset of

a professional leader comes at a cost.

For instance, God endowed all birds with the ability to soar. An eagle is

needed to soar to the highest peak.

Stories also say that if an eagle encounters another bird on the top fly, it must be an eagle. This implies that emulating the eagle requires a certain level of

expense.

Because it necessitates some unavoidable discipline, as mentioned below, true leadership is born in the presence of determination.

1. Discipline with the knowledge that those who are unable to control their spirit will be subjugated by others is the foundation of true leadership.

2. Leadership is a process of self-discovery that manifests in the hearts of people and their surroundings.

3. The development of a mindset that drives change and affects how people behave is what constitutes leadership.

4. The expression of one's inner gift is leadership.

5. The discovery and cultivation of one's potential with an emphasis on the good of all men is leadership.

THE PRINCIPAL APPLICATION OF GREAT LEADERSHIP IS.

1. Selflessness

2. humility

3. Passion

4. Vision

5. Genuine discipline

6. love

7. Persistence.

8. Purpose

CHAPTER FOURTEEN

THE COST OF LEADERSHIP

Think of the greatest teacher of all time, the youthful Jewish rabbi, who was a teacher of the highest calibre and personified our ideal of true leadership. Even his critics and skeptics cannot dispute his passionate life,

for the salvation of mankind, even to the death of the cross.

His impeccable achievement as a leader of the highest order is so deep that It is impossible to conduct a fair study of any historical leader or teacher without mentioning his flawless accomplishments and his role model status

as a teacher of the highest calibre.

No other individual has had such a profound impact on humanity's fate and advancement since the creation of mankind!

He took on the death of the cross for our sake, showing us that progress is impossible without true freedom. His genuine love for the people he had

the honour to lead was the foundation of his leadership.

And because of this love, he offered his life to atone for the sins of the

entire human race. In return for his life, we now enjoy eternal hope,

healing, salvation, freedom, and the deliverance of mankind.

The price of life demands self—the death of a leader.

Genuine Love is the motivation behind true leadership

Any leadership that is not driven by love is manipulative.

The ability to inspire, motivate, mobilize, influence, and especially invite

others to band together and pursue their freedom is what defines true

leadership. while retaining bravery, self-assurance, and dedication.

True Leaders are recognized by their gifts, not by their titles.

What I 'm saying in essence is that a true Leader may not be the most popular person on earth. You don't have to be a leader to be popular. You are not a leader until you have found your calling in life. Until then, you will

exist for the people you were meant to serve with your gifts.

The label of leadership called titles can only make you exist for the people but can never expose you to the reality of effective manifestation. This is

why the greater your leadership the lower the titles.

Meaning to life

Nothing simplifies life and gives it complete direction to set in motion like when someone discovers his gift. It is this that gives life meaning.

A lot of people lead dis—organized, lives, they are confused, doing a lot of things but never becoming experts at any of them. However, to truly release your leadership, you have to focus on one thing and become an

expert at it.

You need to come to the point where only one thing matters most. It is important to note that you are not born to do everything on earth. If you still think you are here to do everything, it means you are yet to discover

your true potential.

I have only one purpose on earth and that has been my motivation every day. As soon as that purpose is accomplished I have finished my work just

like the Apostle Paul. In his second letter to Pastor Timothy.

For I am now ready to be offered, and the time of my departure is at hand.

I have fought a good fight, I have finished my course.

Henceforth there is laid up for me a crown of righteousness, which the Lord, the righteous judge, shall give meat that day: and not to me only, but

unto all them also that love his appearing.

2 Timothy 4:6-48

For many people, life is an illusion, they can tell why they are here. They turn from mountains to Valleys seeking success but as they keep moving

they keep becoming frustrated.

Men and women who realized their life's purpose. live an extraordinarily

meaningful life, for a man's gift, serves as his key to success.

Because it overcomes resistance and thrusts the bearer into the realm of responsibilities.   In other words, a person's gift is the source of his

significance.

• Your gifts make you known before men.

• Gift defines life.

• Your gift is the very you in you!

A clear vision gives you a purpose-driven mindset that is maintained by an optimistic outlook for a better future than the one we currently have. These is what is known as leadership. When you consider this, you'll see why the majority of leaders are constantly reading books and looking for

novel approaches to problems.

CHAPTER FIFTEEN

HOW TO WAKE THE SPIRIT OF LEADERSHIP

When the Spirit of leadership came alive in the life of Moses the man of God, after his encounter with God that produced his conviction. He motivated his Jewish brothers who accepted his vision to follow him even to the point where genuine passion came alive within them too, that they left their Houses, Businesses, jobs,   and Schools in other to follow Moses to the land he told them about. What is your concept of Leadership? A person

is recognized as a leader in his community when his mandate finds expression in the heart of people.

LEADERSHIP BEGINS FROM THE HEART

The concept of leadership is a mental —activity that starts from one's heart and finds expression in the hearts of others motivating them to appreciate and embrace a vision of a future that is better than the present

circumstance. This happened in my life. God started by speaking to my spirit

man till he got me inspired to a vision that became my greatest motivation.

Vision—-driven minds.

These are the reasons why, no matter where you take a trained leader, he will come out leading, because genuine leadership is inborn it doesn't rely on external stimuli. Genuine leaders are internally motivated which is why they are hardly limited by external stimuli.

A person develops an influential outlook on life and the future wherever he finds himself when the spirit of leadership comes alive in him. An impactful attitude is internally developed when this truth becomes real. I begin to realize this wherever I go, first, I realize that, no matter where it is, regardless

of the location. I'm always leading.

This understanding triggered and cultivated within me an influential mindset and attitude. Do you feel the same way too? Then, this book is for you. You need to come to the point where you will realize that you are an impactful leader, designed by the creator to Rule everywhere you go.

Political engagement does not guarantee effective leadership; rather, understanding the behaviorur of strong leaders does. Therefore, we must at least try to scheduled a meeting with a successful leader to find out how they

got to where they are or read about them.

It is an indisputable fact that the creator has endowed each an everyone of us with strong leadership qualities, but activating these abilities demands a price. I think this could be the reason why few individuals are advancing in leadership roles while the majority never think they can. But for you to really lead effectively you must capture and develop the leadership potential within   you.

A careful observer of this truth will understand that the creator first designed us with the capacity to lead, control, and dominate. He did, however, bury this potential within our gift and send us into the world alongside them. Sadly, a lot of these gifts remain imprisoned within us due to a lack of appropriate knowledge and a supportive environment, and we are ultimately responsible for bearing the entire cost necessary for their manifestation. Concerning the narrative that initiates this

discussion, as I previously mentioned:

This is because it debilitates the person's mentality and all the factors that brought those potentials to life, leading them to the wrong paths in life. Then, to make up for their inferiority due to their low self-worth, they will not only oppress others but also intimidate, deceive, and cheat others. This

changes and influences their behaviors negatively.

Though few are aware of this and even fewer think they can manifest it in their communities, all humans are meant to be leaders. But Genuine leadership is something you have to pay the necessary price to discover and

develop before it manifests.

• True Leadership is hidden in a gift.

• True Leadership is not external but inborn.

• True leadership is inside out.

• True leadership starts with the discovery and development of a gift.

• True leadership is self-manifestation to the world.

• True leadership is a self-discovery and distribution to the world.

• True leadership is becoming yourself for others.

When you mentally download certain principles that govern your behaviour and attitude, you start to have the qualities of a real leader. They will be moved to follow you and recognize you as a master as a result of your ability

to inspire and motivate them to behave or act in a particular   way.

www.ingramcontent.com/pod-product-compliance
Lightning Source LLC
Chambersburg PA
CBHW071206290526
45796CB00008B/161